IN THE HOUSE
Turning Your Church Inside Out

Student Leader's Guide

Reach us on the Internet: http://www.reapernet.com

Contents

In The House
Turning Your Church Inside Out

Student Leader's Guide for the 50-Day Spiritual Adventure "The Church You've Always Longed For: What You Can Do to Make It Happen"

Written by Jim Hancock
Editor: Mitch Vander Vorst
Cover Illustration: Bethany Hissong
Text Design: Blum Graphic Design

Copyright ©1996 *The Chapel of the Air Ministries, Inc.*
Published by *The Chapel Ministries*
Dr. David R. Mains, Director

Scripture taken from the HOLY BIBLE, NEW INTERNATIONAL VERSION®. NIV®. Copyright © 1973, 1978, 1984 by International Bible Society. Used by permission of Zondervan Publishing House. All rights reserved.

The Chapel Ministries is a nonprofit, nondenominational, international Christian outreach dedicated to helping God's church grow spiritually and numerically by revitalizing its members, whether they be gathered or scattered, to be a force for kingdom purposes worldwide. To support this goal, The Chapel Ministries provides print and media resources including the annual 50-Day Spiritual Adventure and 4-Week Worship Celebration, the daily half-hour television program "You Need to Know," and seasonal radio programming. Year-round Bible study guides are offered through a Joint Ministry Venture with Scripture Union U.S.A., to encourage the healthy spiritual habits of daily Scripture reading and prayer.

Printed in the United States of America.

ISBN 1-57849-014-6

Introduction

When somebody important is "in the house," everybody gets excited! The show will go on; the star has arrived; let the party begin!

This 50-Day Spiritual Adventure is a celebration that Jesus is *in the house!* It's also an admission that, if he's not in the house, we're kidding ourselves. If Jesus doesn't show up, we may as well go home.

This little book is your guide for the eight meetings that tie together our 50 days of Adventure journaling.

The most important word in the last sentence—I'll wait while you review—the most important word in the last sentence is the word *together*. We journal alone, then we meet together. That's because, in the goodness of God, we're *in the house* together. The work of Jesus is for each of us and for all of us—together. My favorite part of the last 50-Day Adventure was the honesty and understanding that emerged in our little group over the course of eight weeks. We were, I think, more together at the end than we were in the beginning. And it's making a difference in our group.

The Theme

This Adventure explores what happens when Jesus is in the house. The eight themes in this Student Leader's Guide expand on the weekly Adventure themes in the Student Journal. The 50-Day Spiritual Adventure includes eight Sundays but only seven full weeks. (Themes 7 and 8 are combined in the last week.) If you meet on Sundays, your Session 1 will be on Day 1 of the Adventure. If you meet on a weekday, your Session 1 will be sometime during the first week (Days 1–6 of the Adventure). It breaks down like this:

When Jesus Is in the House:

Theme 1:	**Everybody matters** Student Journal Days 1–6
Theme 2:	**You can bring your friends** Student Journal Days 7–13
Theme 3:	**It's okay to be me** Student Journal Days 14–20
Theme 4:	**We help each other be all we can be** Student Journal Days 21–27
Theme 5:	**People are real** Student Journal Days 28–34
Theme 6:	**We make a difference** Student Journal Days 35–41
Theme 7:	**God shows up** Student Journal Days 42–46
Theme 8:	**The future looks bright** Student Journal Days 47–50

Get the Movie

In the House: Excerpts from EdgeTV

If you like the book, you'll love the movie. Each session in this guide suggests a video segment from In the House: Excerpts from EdgeTV.

EdgeTV is the video magazine for youth groups. Unlike other videos you may be used to, there are no easy answers on EdgeTV. The segments are short and open-ended—designed to help get kids talking. And they will talk, once you convince them they'll be heard. The sessions in this guide stand up nicely without the video segments, but In the House: Excerpts from EdgeTV will bump your 50-Day Spiritual Adventure up a notch.

To order your copy of In the House: Excerpts from EdgeTV *or any other Adventure resource use the order form on page 64 in this leader's guide.*

Action!

There are five action steps and a couple of other assignments in the 50-Day Spiritual Adventure. They are outlined more completely on pages 6–12 of the Student Journal. If you follow the session plans in this guide, you'll cover all the action step assignments from the Student Journal. In most cases, the assigned action steps are incorporated as applications of the session material. These are the activities your students will be involved in during the Adventure:

every day

• **READ** the assigned Scripture passages and answer the questions in the journal.

• **ACTION STEP 1: Get Your Ears Pierced** (p. 6 of the Student Journal). Pray the Pierced Ears Prayer using the words on page 7 of the Student Journal (there is a reproducible prayer on p. 13 of this guide).

• **ACTION STEP 2: Catch the Rave** (p. 8 of the Student Journal). Write down something good about your youth group or church. And once a week, rave to a friend about your youth group or church. Also, invite someone to church or youth group before the Adventure is over.

every week

• **READ** the appropriate chapter in Dan Lupton's book *I Like Church, But . . .*

twice

• **ACTION STEP 3: Cross the Lines** (p. 9 of the Student Journal). Get together with two people outside your normal circle of friends.

once

• **ACTION STEP 4: Electrify a Friend** (p. 11 of the Student Journal). Help bring out someone's potential.

• **ACTION STEP 5: Take Out the Trash** (p. 12 of the Student Journal). Throw out some trash from your life.

It takes skill to make a group work. Not everybody likes groups. For example, some of us are what we call "shy." Shyness doesn't have to be a problem because still waters run deep and, if we connect with shy people, their depth can be a tremendous asset to the group. But we have to work to make it safe for introverts to participate. Be assured of this: If the shy people get into it, everybody will get into it.

• If your group is large, consider forming smaller teams before beginning the Adventure. Smaller is better for shy folk. If you usually start your meetings with singing or ice-breakers, go right ahead and do that during the Adventure. Note that there are video segments from *In the House: Excerpts from EdgeTV* and sometimes readings at the beginning of each session. These are designed to ramp your group into the content of the session.

• Establish a no-fluff zone around your group process. Ask everyone to avoid getting sucked into meaningless chatter during the sessions and to agree to refocus quickly if someone points out that the group is drifting.

• Ask everyone to agree to confidentiality in the group. "What you see here, what you say here, let it stay here when you leave here."

• Be a participant. Go through the Student Journal yourself and spend time doing all the action steps. If you don't engage in this Adventure—if you don't take the lead by talking about your own struggles—no one else will want to go first. And that's what has to happen if your group is going to be safe enough for kids to open up—someone has to go first. You can be that person. I think you *should* be that person. But, for goodness sake, don't just talk about struggles that happened when you were a kid. Let your group know that you're on the road with them right now—maybe a few miles ahead, but definitely still on the road. If kids know that you need Jesus, right here, right now, they'll be encouraged to consider their own need.

• You don't have to be the Lone Ranger. In fact, it's better if you're not. See what you can do to involve kids and other adults in the 50-Day Spiritual Adventure. Ask someone to help you with the readings. Get a video assistant to cue the videotape and handle the lights. Invite others to tell their own stories of life with Christ: When it comes to expressing our honest need for Christ, you don't always have to go first if another adult or student will take the lead. They're probably willing to be asked.

It probably goes without saying (but I'll say it anyway): People get more out of the Adventure if they go through the journal. Take time to preview the Student Journal with your group the week before the Adventure begins. Explain the action steps and hand out Adventure materials.

Each adventurer should have his or her own copy of the Student Journal and access to the book *I Like Church, But . . .* by Dan Lupton (also available on audiocassette). To obtain these materials (and *In the House: Excerpts from EdgeTV*), contact The Chapel Ministries at 1-800-224-2735 (U.S.) or 1-800-461-4114 (Canada), visit your local Christian bookstore, or use the order form in the back of this guide.

I'm excited that Jesus *is* in the house! And I'm asking God to bless you as you begin this new Adventure and to help your group members turn your church inside out.

How Do You Feel When People Talk Down To You?

I feel bad when people talk down to me. So I work hard at not talking down to kids, and I've prepared this guide with that in mind. I urge you to lead your group through these studies without flinching. If you wonder if they're following a particular idea, ask them. If you give them permission, they'll tell you when they feel lost. If they are lost, you can gently lead them back onto the path.

Meanwhile, don't be afraid of silence. If it goes on too long, ask what it means: Are you thinking? Are you confused? Do I need to ask the question another way? Ask and you will receive. . . .

Preparation

You'll notice that this material is undated so you can use it during any seven-week (eight-Sunday) period you choose. A lot of people will use the Adventure materials to finish on Easter Sunday, or during the 50 days leading to Pentecost. This Adventure was made for you, not you for this Adventure—make it work for you.

Get familiar with the Student Journal and the book *I Like Church, But* . . . Read the introductory pages of the Student Journal (pp. 3–12) and skim the rest of the journal to acquaint yourself with the daily format and the eight topics.

If kids participate, there's no way you can use all the material from this guide in an hour. You'll have to choose the options that fit your time requirements. Choosing wisely usually means choosing in advance.

There are four main parts to each session:

• Video: each session suggests a clip from *In The House: Excerpts from EdgeTV* and provides focus and follow-up questions.

• Readings: five sessions include readings from other sources.

• Bible Study: each session includes Bible study texts, introductions, and questions.

• Action Steps: each session will inform you of what action steps your kids will be involved in. You will need to remind them of their assignments and keep them on track.

Don't worry about fitting everything in. You can pick and choose what works best for you. You can use the readings, or not. You can ask all the questions, or pick the ones you think work best in your situation. Let your specific time restrictions and group culture dictate how you use this guide. You may want to use some parts in Sunday school and others during your midweek youth group. Or you may want to develop small groups that use some parts of this guide at other times. The key is, it's all up to you. The important thing to remember, though, is to make sure you maintain a balance and keep everything focused on the themes your students will be doing on their own in their Student Journals. And remember: You're the expert when it comes to knowing your group.

Further Preparation

• Take time to read through each session several days in advance so you can be prepared.

• Some sessions call for pencil and paper and materials.

• If possible, get everyone in the same version of the Bible. I've used the New International Version in my preparation, but you can use whatever you have.

• Some sessions include lengthy Bible passages or readings from books. That's a great opportunity to involve kids or other leaders. Get your readers together before the session to run through the passages. A few minutes of work can turn those readings into important moments in your group. A little drama goes a long way.

• Some book quotes were too long to include in this guide. The quotes are from *The Screwtape Letters* and *Mere Christianity* by C. S. Lewis and *Where the Sidewalk Ends* by Shel Silverstein. If you have copies of these books, make sure you bring them to your meeting. If you don't, check your church or local public library.

Before Day 1 of the Adventure, be certain that your students understand what they need to do daily, weekly, and in general throughout the Adventure time. The action step descriptions are on pages 6–12 of the Student Journal, and a preview of all the action steps is on page 5 of the Student Journal. You will want to keep up with all the assignments yourself. The action steps are a big part of this Adventure, and missing out on them is just plain missing out. You may want to weave some of the action steps into your meetings—doing them together as a group. Or you may wish to plan special outings or meetings in which you can help facilitate the action steps.

The main thing is not to let your group forget about the action steps. Keep reminding them each week of what assignments they should be keeping up with. Ask for progress reports. And try to build some sort of accountability into it all.

On the following page are a few ideas you can use in a pre-Adventure meeting, before you begin the eight sessions in this guide.

If you can, take some time before the 50-Day Spiritual Adventure begins for pre-Adventure meetings. These ideas will help you familiarize your group with the action steps in this Adventure.

Pass out the Student Journals and make sure there is enough scratch paper and plenty of pencils to go around.

Get Your Ears Pierced

Read through the Pierced Ears Prayer on page 7 of the Student Journal. Have students write the prayer out in their own words, then share it with the group. The prayer is also printed on page 13 of this guide. You have our permission to reproduce it and pass it out to your group.

Catch the Rave

Invite everyone to write down something your group does well or a good time you've had together. Pile their responses together and read them out loud. You may find that one person's response draws groans from someone else. If so, ask if it's good news or bad news that your group is broad enough to include people who aren't always alike.

Cross the Lines

Ask everyone to pair off and take two minutes to make a quick list of the lines that divide people in their schools and neighborhoods. Compile their lists on a board or overhead.

Electrify a Friend

Ask everyone if they can recall a time when someone made them feel like they could be great at something. What is it like to feel that way (or what's it like never to feel that way)?

Take Out the Trash

Take nominations for the messiest bedroom, car, or school locker in the group. If you have time in advance, get parents, siblings, or friends to sneak a Polaroid snapshot or a few seconds of videotape of someone's bedroom, car, or locker for the group to enjoy. After the fun, ask if anybody ever feels as if their *life* is messy like that. What would it be like to clean up your life?

Also: Show your group the Guidebook (or Audio Guidebook) *I Like Church, But . . .* by Dan Lupton. Let them know that they can enhance their Adventure even more by reading (or listening to) this book, and tell them how to get their own copies.

Direct everyone to the warm-up days on pages 13–14 of the Student Journal. Encourage them to take a few minutes Friday and Saturday to do those pages, or go through them together.

Close your pre-Adventure meeting by asking God to help each of you—and all of you together—let Jesus turn your youth group inside out.

the pierced ears prayer

Lord,

i WAnt To LOVe
pEoPlE THE wAY YOU do,

But SoMEtiMeS iT's liKE i Don't
EVEN heAr WhaT ThEy'RE
saYiNg.

PlEAsE TeACh mE tO liSTen
wItH Your ears.

i PRAy For: _____.

a need you've heard recently

lORd, hElP me TO bE AN EvEn
BeTtER LISTEneR,

AND ShOw Me if i cAn do
anyThiNG To HeLP.

amen.

THEME 1

When Jesus is in the house . . . everybody matters

Days 1–6 in the Student Journal

GOALS:
- To invite your group into the 50-Day Spiritual Adventure
- To create an atmosphere that says, "This won't be business as usual"
- To affirm that in your group everybody matters

READ:
"The Real World"

Read or have someone read this excerpt from Scott Greenberg's Senior Speech at the 1988 Torrey Pines High School graduation in Del Mar, California:

> I came home from school after having a really bad day. I had failed a few tests, got beaten up, and some other things, and I said to my father, "Dad, let me tell ya something about life. It's a jungle out there! Nothing but problems and headaches and people on your back. It's like a roller coaster; sometimes you're up, but eventually you'll come down and stay down. Life is a miserable thing."
>
> My father looked at me and said, "Scott, let me tell you something about life. You think you have problems now? You don't have a house to pay off, a car to pay off. You don't have a family to feed or a business to run. You think you have problems now? Just wait until you get out into the real world."
>
> Wait until I get out into the real world? Well, I think I'm pretty much speaking for the entire senior class when I ask a very simple question to the parents out there: What the hell is the real world?! Is this actually a place with people?
>
> I just don't understand! And the worst part about it is, if I'm not in the real world, where am I? I must be in some cosmic, metaphysical state of existence, somewhere between Never Never Land and Hell. It's very confusing.
>
> So we ask, "What exactly is the real world?" and we're told, "The real world is a place of problems, anxieties and headaches." Well, if this is the case—that the real world is a place with problems, anxieties and headaches—then, ladies and gentlemen, I have been to the real world because I have been to high school.

Talk:

1. What feelings does Scott's speech raise for you?

2. Have you ever gotten the kind of lecture Scott got from his dad? What was that like?

3. Are there any points at which you disagree with Scott?

4. What is your gut reaction when people act like just because you're young you don't know anything?

VIEW:

In The House! Excerpts from EdgeTV
"(dis)Respect" from EdgeTV 18
14.5 minutes

"I try to respect others as much as I respect myself."

People need respect as desperately as they need food, water, and air. Any day you can see people dying for lack of respect, and other people fight like drowning men to get or keep respect. It's amazing how much the drive for respect lies behind youth violence, drugs, sex, and so many of the ills we wring our hands about. Your group probably contains someone who is starving for respect, as well as quite a few students who are surviving on short rations. This segment gives you an opportunity to check out how full your students' respect fuel tanks are, as well as to encourage greater respect among group members. The world is full of people and situations that tear down our self-respect. Your group can be a safe place to build one another up in this crucial area.

Focus Question:

Before turning on the tape  ask students to tell what the word respect means to them. How do they know when s _____ _____ them to watch the tape and listen for statements t _____ _____ of he may disagree with.

After reading + questions, before video.

Follow-up Questions:

1. a. What did you hear _____ that you agreed with?

    b. What did you hear _____ hat you disagreed with?

2. What wins respect for a _____ guy in your neighborhood? What wins respect for a girl? (Money, looks, grades, rea _____ ness, faith, integrity, honesty, generosity, kindness, talent?
Make some lists. Are these _____ things that "should" win respect? Where do these standards come from?)

3. Pass out cards and pencils, and have students write numbers for each item. Then discuss them.

   a. On a scale of 0 to 5, how much do you respect yourself? Your parents? Teachers? Other people?

   b. On a scale of 0 to 5, how much respect do you feel you get from your peers? Parents? Teachers?

4. Do you feel like most people you meet respect you? What makes you feel that way?

5. What do you feel when someone disrespects you? What do you do?

6. Many kids have never been taught how to respond to disrespect without either retreating or attacking. In many neighborhoods, it is customary to become violent with people who show disrespect; those who do not fight for their honor lose respect from everyone and suffer for it. Try some role plays in which you demonstrate how you would respond to disrespect from a peer. First ask a group member to play an adult who is rude to you in a store. Perhaps someone who cuts in line ahead of you. Demonstrate how you might respectfully challenge that person's behavior without encouraging tempers to flare. If this is hard for you, tell your group. They will benefit from hearing about your own struggles to treat yourself and others with respect even in a situation of conflict. Then ask students to role play a similar situation. One person disrespects the other. How should the other respond in a way that shows respect for herself and the first person?

7. Who do you respect, and why?

8. Are there groups of people whom you find it hard to respect? Blacks? Whites? Agents? People with disabilities? Adults? Why?

9. One of the guys in the video (Drey) won no respect for being himself, so he turned to dealing drugs in order to win respect for his money. Does this make sense to you? Is respect important enough that a person should do whatever it takes to get respect? What would you say to him if he were your friend?

10. Why is respect so essential that we will do such drastic things to get it?

11. Drey says what he really wants is for a real friend to respect him even when he falls. Is that what you want? Why?

12. How did knowing Jesus help some of the people in the video handle disrespect from others? How did knowing Jesus help build their self-respect?

13. a. The girl (Zoey) said she would like to be able to draw her self-respect from Jesus, but she is honest enough to admit she hasn't been able to do that. How does a person learn to draw self-respect from Jesus? Does this happen by magic, or do we need to do something?

b. Why do you think being forced to have sex as a small child made her lose respect for herself, even though it wasn't her fault?

c. Do you ....

14. Read in Luke .... think it's so great to be disr......

15. Read in John .... could have struck all of his .... What does this scene tell you about hi... If you did this, do you think people wou ... adult S.S. class?

16. If you've alwa .... pain of people who haver ...

17. Do you feel lik .... atening question. Have you .... people in this group let you ...

18. One guy (Lew) s .... because I'm a person I don't want to be." Do you think God wants us to feel that way? Explain. Consider Romans 8:1–2.

[handwritten note overlapping text:] How would any of you feel having to go down + teach an adult S.S. class? Like Timothy?

BIBLE STUDY:
1 Timothy 4:1–5:2

Paul is writing to his partner in ministry, a young man named Timothy. We don't know how young Timothy was, but we know he had to lead people a lot older than he was through some difficult problems.

• Read or have someone read 1 Timothy 4:1–5:2.
• Invite everyone to reflect for a moment on what they've heard as if they had never heard it before.

Talk:
1. Does this passage raise any questions for you?

2. What kinds of things is Timothy supposed to help the church deal with?

3. Are there such things in the church today? How would you like to be responsible for solving those problems?

4. In verses 7–9, what preparation does Paul recommend to Timothy?

5. Look at verses 4:11–5:2.
   a. What is Timothy supposed to do?

   b. How is he to conduct his relationships?

6. Let's go back and focus on verse 12. Paul says don't let anyone look down on you because you are young, but be an example for the believers—young and old—in what you say. What do you think that means? Go to Ephesians 4:29–32; James 1:19; and 1 Peter 3:15 for clues.

7. Be an example for the believers in what you do. What do you think that means? Go to Ephesians 4:17–28 for clues.

8. Be an example for the believers in how you love. What do you think that means? Go to John 15:9–17 for clues.

9. Be an example for the believers in the quality of your faith. What do you think that means? Go to Luke 12:22–31 for clues.

10. And be an example for the believers in holiness. What do you think that means? Go to 1 Thessalonians 4:3–8 and 1 Peter 1:13–16 for clues.

11. Is there anything else that stands out for you in this passage from 1 Timothy?

TAKING STEPS:

Take time to make sure your group understands their action step assignments from the Student Journal. (See p. 6 in this guide and pp. 5–12 in the Student Journal.) If you didn't have a pre-Adventure meeting you may need to introduce them to the assignments. The action step to emphasize this first week is Action Step 1—Get your ears pierced. But you will also want to make sure your group is tracking with Action Step 2.

1. What's the most significant thing you've heard or thought in this session?

2. Why is that so significant to you?

3. What do you think you—or we—might do about that?

4. How does "getting your ears pierced" help anything?

Each Day This Week:

1. If everybody matters, then each one of us matters. Can we ask God to help us treat each other as if we mattered in this group? Pray the Pierced Ears Prayer using the words on page 7 of the Student Journal as a guide.

2. Will you make an effort to study the assigned Scripture passages and answer the questions in the journal this week?

3. Will you try to "catch the rave" and write down something good about our youth group or church every day this week?

Once This Week:

1. Read chapter 1 in Dan Lupton's book *I Like Church, But . . .*

2. Rave to a friend about our youth group or church.

PRAY:

Pray that our group will come to believe that everybody matters here.

Notes

Start now praying about and looking
for someone that you can invite to
church or youth group.

THEME 2

When Jesus is in the house . . . you can bring your friends

Days 7–13 in the Student Journal

GOALS:
- To encourage your group in their 50-Day Spiritual Adventure
- To acknowledge what God has begun
- To affirm the presence of Christ in your group

VIEW:

In The House! Excerpts from EdgeTV
"Why I'm Not a Christian" from EdgeTV 4
3ish minutes

"This stuff about Jesus scares me—nobody ever explained it."

Marcy was raised in a churchgoing home, and from what she says here, you can tell she's had at least some teaching on the gospel. But something hasn't clicked. Chances are high that somebody in your group feels like Marcy and may not have dared to say so. You can provide a forum for that person to raise honest questions and get answers that make sense.

One reason why many church-bred kids don't understand the gospel is that it's explained to them in words that mean little to them. "Lexicon-o-rama" from EdgeTV Edition 4 could help you there.

The first two questions below would also make good focus questions.

Follow-up Questions:
1. What do you think of Marcy's beliefs?

2. Do you know anybody like Marcy?

3. What would you say to Marcy if she were your friend?

4. What would be some *wrong* ways to respond to Marcy?

5. Marcy doesn't understand why Jesus "had to die to save us from our sins." Old Testament images of blood sacrifice seem bizarre to many people, and many don't see why God couldn't forgive us without sending Jesus.

What parts of your church's teaching do you think would be hard to explain to non-Christians in your school? Why would those be hard?

6. How would you explain why Jesus had to die? Avoid Christian jargon like *justification*, *repentance*, or *righteousness*. If you do use a word that non-Christians misunderstand, such as sin or grace, explain it in terms that an average modern person would understand.

(To give everyone a chance at this, divide your group into triads. One person can give an explanation, and the others can question him or her as though they're non-Christians who really want to understand. Listen to the explanations and questions; they'll point to topics you need to teach on and areas in which your students may have been misunderstanding you.)

BIBLE STUDY:
1 Peter 3:8–12

Peter offers practical advice to clusters of believers scattered across the Mediterranean world about 30 years after the resurrection of Jesus.

• Read or have someone read 1 Peter 3:8–12.

Write:
Take the next four minutes to rewrite this passage in your own words.

Talk:
1. How do you feel about this passage? Why is that?

2. Peter creates quite a list of behaviors for the church here: harmony, sympathy, love, compassion, humility, repaying evil and insult with blessing.

   a. Which of these actions is easiest for you? Why do you think that is?

   b. Which of these actions is most difficult for you? Why do you think that is?

3. Verses 10–12 are quoted from Psalm 34. Is there anything that makes it difficult for you to "seek peace and pursue it" in our church? Can you tell us about that?

4. How easy is it to invite your friends to our group? Why?

5. How easy is it to invite your friends to this church? Why?

6. What would make it easier for you to bring your friends here? Is that something we can fix?

READ:

Read of have someone read chapter II from *The Screwtape Letters* by C. S. Lewis (Collier Books, Macmillan Publishing Company; New York: 1959, pp. 11–14).

Talk:

1. What strikes you about this passage from *The Screwtape Letters?*

2. Do you agree with Screwtape when he writes: "All the habits of the patient, both mental and bodily, are still in our favour"? Why?

3. How about when he says, "One of our great allies at present is the Church itself"? Why do you think that?

4. What do you make of Screwtape's distinction between the church on the corner and the "invisible" church?

5. As honestly as you can, describe the range of your attitudes about the people in this church. (You don't need to name names.)

   a. Are there people here with whom you're uncomfortable? Why?

   b. Are there people you're surprised to see here? Why?

   c. Are there people who—as a gut reaction—you don't think belong here? What do you mean?

6. Are you aware of any ways in which the devil tempts you to think or act ungenerously towards other people in the church? Can you tell us about that?

7. Have you found yourself speaking ungenerously about other people in the church? Can you tell us about that?

Write:

Take the next four minutes to write a note to God about your place in this group and in this church. What do you wish God would do?

TAKING STEPS:

Take time to make sure your group understands their action step assignments from the Student Journal. (See p. 6 in this guide and pp. 5–12 in the Student Journal.) The action step to emphasize this week is Action Step 2—Catch the rave. But you will also want to make sure your group is still tracking with Action Step 1.

1. What's the most significant thing you've heard or thought in this session?

2. Why is that so significant to you?

3. What do you think you—or we—might do about that?

4. How can our group "catch the rave"?

Each Day This Week:

1. People outside our group only have what we say about each other to go on. Can we ask God to help us treat each other as generously as we would like to be treated in this group? Pray the Pierced Ears Prayer using the words on page 7 of the Student Journal as a guide.

2. Will you make an effort to study the assigned Scripture passages and answer the questions in the journal this week?

3. Will you try to "catch the rave" and write down something good about our youth group or church every day this week?

Once This Week:

1. Read chapter 2 in Dan Lupton's book *I Like Church, But . . .*

2. Rave to a friend about our youth group or church.

PRAY:

Pray that our group will learn to celebrate the body of Christ.

Notes

_____

_____

_____

_____

_____

_____

_____

_____

_____

THEME 3

Session •3•

When Jesus is in the house . . . it's okay to be me

Days 14–20 in the Student Journal

GOALS:
• To acknowledge that God loves everyone
• To deepen your group's commitment to love those whom God loves

READ:
"The Long-Haired Boy"

Read or have someone read "The Long-Haired Boy" from *Where the Sidewalk Ends* by Shel Silverstein (Harper and Row; New York: 1974, pp. 137–139).

Talk:
1. What feelings does "The Long-Haired Boy" bring up for you?

2. Is there someone like the Long-Haired Boy at your school?

3. Have you been in the kind of place that boy was in? Can you tell us about that?

4. Why, do you think, are there insiders and outsiders in society?

5. Why, do you think, are there insiders and outsiders in the church?

6. The Long-Haired Boy was an outsider just because he had long hair. But some people are outsiders—not because of something superficial—because they did wrong. What do you think is a godly attitude toward those people?

VIEW:

In The House! Excerpts from EdgeTV
"Germaine" from EdgeTV 11
9:25 minutes

"I used sex to buy what I wanted."

At last the woman you've all been waiting for: Germaine Peters! If you're new to EdgeTV, then you don't know that Germaine has been the subject of rumor and speculation ever since "Double Play" (EdgeTV Edition 7). In subsequent editions those who know her have declined to talk, but now Germaine speaks. Some questions remain unanswered (Did she or did she not do it with Trevin?), but some of the really important issues have become a little clearer.

Focus Question:

If your group has been following the story begun in "Double Play," then before you turn on the tape, invite students to describe what they think Germaine is probably like. (This discussion could start to get out of hand, so cut it off after a couple of minutes.)

If your group has not been following our story—what's the matter with you? (Sure, this conversation with Germaine stands perfectly well on its own, but do you know what you've missed?)

By the way, when we shot this segment, young women in the cast and crew spent painful nights because Germaine's story is their story. Their pain is redemptive because all three of them are making strides toward stories that could qualify for our "Great Comebacks" segment. But if three members of our team recognized themselves in Germaine, chances are high that you have a Germaine or two in your group. Make sure that at some point during this session you invite any and all Germaines to speak with you or some other adult privately to help solve the issues that have put them where they are.

Follow-up Questions:

1. What are you thinking after watching that?

2. Were you surprised by Germaine, or was she about what you expected? Explain.

3. Why was Germaine sexually active? What were her motives?

4. How typical do you think Germaine is of other young women who are sexually active in their teens? Why do you say that?

5. Why would a girl use sex as money? (Does that seem totally incomprehensible to you, or can you think of reasons in the rest of her life that might make that make sense?)

6. If you were in a class with Germaine, how would you relate to her? (That is, how do you typically relate to people like Germaine?) Why?

7. What do you think about a guy who buys what a girl like Germaine is selling? Explain. (You might ask the girls in your group to keep quiet on this one and let the guys answer. Or, have students write their answers along with their gender on index cards, then pass them in and compare how each gender views the matter.)

8. a. How does God view Germaine? Is she "ruined"? Dirty? See John 7:53–8:11 or Luke 7:36–50.

    b. Based on the passage you just read, what do you think Jesus would say to Germaine? What would he do? What would he want Germaine to do?

9. In Matthew 11:28–30, Jesus tells people in Germaine's situation to take his "yoke" on them. (That's *yoke*, not *yolk*.) You might want to explain that a yoke is something you put on a pair of oxen so they can plow together. Okay, so maybe they don't have oxen where you live. But imagine that you have to drag a large, heavy object (like your life), and the only way you can do this is to hitch yourself together with somebody who knows what they're doing so they can share the load and set the pace.

    What would it look like for Germaine to take on Jesus' yoke—to plow with him and learn from him? What would that look like in practice for her?

10. If Germaine told you her story, what would you say and do? What do you have that Germaine needs?

11. What would you say to Germaine's mom?

12. a. What do you think Germaine's next move will be?

    b. What do you think it *should* be?

For Further Information:

In "Sexual Choices" (Edge TV Edition 2), we heard from several real-life young women who made the same kinds of choices Germaine made. Also, in "Addictive Behavior" (EdgeTV Edition 3), we learned that sexual behavior can be called an addiction when it (a) is done to handle struggle or sorrow, (b) impairs one's ability to love others, and (c) cannot be stopped without extensive outside intervention. One could certainly apply "a" and "b" to Germaine's activity, while one could debate "c."

BIBLE STUDY:
Luke 15:1–32

Jesus is on the road, telling everyone who will listen about the kingdom of God. Some people—especially people who know they're in trouble—like what they hear. But the mainstream religious folk aren't buying it.

- Read or have someone read Luke 15:1–32.
- Invite everyone to reflect for a moment on what they've heard as if they had never heard it before.

Talk:

1. What do these three parables have in common?

2. Is it just me, or is there something strange about these stories?

   a. What's the sense in risking 99 sheep in order to find one that's lost?

   b. What's the sense in taking back a runaway kid—no questions asked? (Especially when there's a quite obedient first child who stayed put and never did anything bad!)

3. Are there some lost sheep loose in our community?

   a. What do you think would happen if our pastor turned the worship service over to a substitute and went after those lost sheep?

   b. What do you think would happen if we went out of our way to go after the lost sheep at school and in the community?

4. Are there some lost coins hidden in our church—people with plenty of value that we can't seem to get our hands on?

   a. What would it take to light a lamp, sweep the house, and search carefully until we found those people?

   b. What do you suppose keeps us from taking the trouble to find the lost coins?

5. Do you know of some lost sons and daughters—people who have turned their backs on our heavenly Father and are misusing his gifts to them?

   a. As honestly as you can now, case by case: Is your attitude closer to the waiting father or the older brother? Why?

   b. What would it take for you to welcome each of them home?

TAKING STEPS:

Take time to make sure your group understands their action step assignments from the Student Journal. (See p. 6 in this guide and pp. 5–12 in the Student Journal.) The action step to emphasize this week is Action Step 3—Cross the lines. But you will also want to make sure your group is still tracking with Action Steps 1 and 2.

1. What's the most significant thing you've heard or thought in this session?

2. Why is that so significant to you?

3. What do you think you—or we—might do about that?

4. How can our group "cross the lines"?

Each Day This Week:

1. If it's okay for me to be me, then it's okay for you to be you. Can we ask God to help us deal with each other where we are instead of where we should be—and then move together toward where we should be? Pray the Pierced Ears Prayer using the words on page 7 of the Student Journal as a guide.

2. Will you make an effort to study the assigned Scripture passages and answer the questions in the journal this week?

3. Will you try to "catch the rave" and write down something good about our youth group or church every day this week?

Once This Week:

1. Read chapter 3 in Dan Lupton's book *I Like Church, But . . .*

2. Rave to a friend about our youth group or church.

Before the Adventure Is Over:

1. Cross the lines and get together with two people outside your normal circle of friends: a lost sheep, a lost coin, a lost daughter or son. Consider people of different race, ethnicity, socioeconomic status, and so on, or people in a different clique or group.

PRAY:

Pray that our group will look past differences to see people as Jesus sees them.

Notes

THEME 4

When Jesus is in the house . . . we help each other be all we can be

Days 21–27 in the Student Journal

GOALS:
- To encourage each group member to be all he or she was created to be
- To demonstrate ways your group can encourage each other

VIEW:
In the House! Excerpts from EdgeTV
"PFR" from EdgeTV 15
13ish minutes

"I like what they do to my life."

PFR used to abbreviate the real name of this band: Pray for Rain. Turned out somebody was already using that name and the abbreviation stuck. Since then, PFR have sold a boat-load of records, been included in an all-star salute to the Beatles, and gotten serious mainstream attention in Europe. They write songs that are real and almost unbelievably rich with musical hooks.

PFR love kids. We caught up with them at Camp Shamineau, where they've worked and sung for years (and where Pat began his life with Christ). Mark spent the summer of 1995 as Program Director at camp, serving kids and getting centered on Christ. Joel was at Shamineau with his wife, Kathy the Nature Lady, looking for ways to encourage the camp staff. Pat, newly married to Helen, spent the summer in Minneapolis getting to know his bride. All three were very thoughtful about the upcoming PFR tour.

By the way, you may recognize Mark from "Fear " in episode 15 of EdgeTV. We didn't make a big deal about it in that story because, after all, we really are all in this together, aren't we? We mention it here so you'll know and have the chance to tie the two together if you want to.

Joel, Pat, and Mark are extraordinarily generous guys who tell their stories with grace and hope. They are at a point where hiding out would be safe for their image but damaging to their spirits. So they've stepped up to the plate to tell the truth about their walk with Christ in all its splendor and all its struggle. If we had hats, they'd be raised to PFR.

Focus Question:

What is your image of life on the road for Christians playing in a band? Where did you get that image? What makes you believe it's true?

Follow-up Questions:

1. What do you think of these guys?

2. Being in a hot band may seem like a dream come true, but it's not without its price. What struggles and temptations do the guys of PFR face because of their work?

3. What do they do to handle those struggles and temptations?

4. What do you think of the idea of having some friends who you come clean with, friends who can point their fingers in your face and say, "Are you where you need to be?" What would be the advantages and disadvantages of friends like that?

5. Why would Joel say that the more he's told his close friends about the lousy things he's done, the more freedom he's found? Why would that be true?

6. Read Galatians 6:1–5. How is this like what Mark, Pat, and Joel describe doing with their friends?

7. Were you surprised that what these guys are hungry for is quiet places to settle down with their wives? Why?

8. Mark's goal is to develop a mature faith that doesn't threaten non-Christians. Why doesn't mature faith threaten non-Christians?

9. What do you think of their view of success: being somebody even when they're not great musicians anymore? Why do you suppose inner character is so important to these guys?

BIBLE STUDY:
Ephesians 4:1–16

Paul has just offered his prayer for every believer and given glory to the God who is able to do more in each of us than we can even imagine. Now he explores our responsibility to each other.

• Read or have someone read Ephesians 4:1–16.
• Invite everyone to reflect for a moment on what they've heard as if they had never heard it before.

Talk:

1. What would you say are the big ideas in Ephesians 4:1–6?

2. There's a big "but" at the beginning of verse 7. "But" what?
(Don't get tripped up by the parenthetical remark about Jesus ascending and descending. The point is the contrast between all of us in verse 6 and each of us in verse 7. God is over all and through all and in all, but each of us gets grace in the form of gifts that benefit the family of God.)

3. In verse 11, what kinds of gifts to the church does Paul identify?

   a. Go to Paul's lists in Romans 12:3–8 and 1 Corinthians 12:4–11 and 27–31. Add them to the list in Ephesians 4.

   b. Where have you seen some of these gifts in action?

   c. Can you see any indication that some of these gifts may be emerging from the people in this room? Tell us about that.

4. Go to 1 Corinthians 12:12–26. Compare these verses with what we read in Ephesians 4:15–16.

   a. What are these gifts for?

   b. What is the ultimate goal?

5. How can we help each other grow up into Christ, the Head of the body? Go to Hebrews 10:23–25 for a clue.

TAKING STEPS:

Take time to make sure your group understands their action step assignments from the Student Journal. (See p. 6 in this guide and pp. 5–12 in the Student Journal.) The action step to emphasize this week is Action Step 4—Electrify a friend. But you will also want to make sure your group is still tracking with Action Steps 1–3.

1. What's the most significant thing you've heard or thought in this session?

2. Why is that so significant to you?

3. What do you think you—or we—might do about that?

4. What can our group do to make sure we help each other be all we can be?

Each Day this Week:

1. It takes all of us to grow into the fullness of Christ. Can we ask God to help us encourage each other as if we really meant it? Pray the Pierced Ears Prayer using the words on page 7 of the Student Journal as a guide.

2. Will you make an effort to study the assigned Scripture passages and answer the questions in the journal this week?

3. Will you try to "catch the rave" and write down something good about our youth group or church every day this week?

Once This Week:

1. Read chapter 4 in Dan Lupton's book *I Like Church, But* . . .

2. Rave to a friend about youth group or church.

Before the Adventure Is Over:

1. Empower someone—electrify a friend and help bring out his or her potential.

PRAY:

Pray that our group will become a place of encouragement, growth, and celebration for positive change.

Notes

_____
_____
_____
_____
_____
_____
_____
_____
_____
_____
_____
_____
_____
_____
_____
_____
_____
_____
_____
_____
_____
_____
_____
_____
_____
_____

Session •5•

THEME 5

When Jesus is in the house . . . people are real

Days 28–34 in the Student Journal

GOALS:
• To make your group safer for honest and appropriate self-disclosure
• To encourage and celebrate real progress

VIEW:
In the House! Excerpts from EdgeTV
"Meet the Fines" from EdgeTV 14
4ish minutes

"I don't know what he's talking about. There's nothing wrong; everything's FINE."

Meet the Fines. A happy family if ever there was one, taking Serenity out for her birthday. Tension? Manipulation? No ma'am, the Fines are just FINE. "What's that odor in the living room?" you ask. Oh, pay no attention to that. The Fines don't. Chester simply smokes his pipe so he can't smell it, while Serenity wears nose plugs.

What kind of a family ignores an elephant inhabiting their living room, leaving odoriferous (that's an SAT word for "smelly") tokens at regular intervals? Maybe you know a family like that; maybe some of your students live in one. Lots of families pretend everything's fine at home, ignoring problems as large as a pachyderm in the parlor.

Focus Question:
The central characters in this story are Serenity Fine, her brother Chip, and her parents, Celeste and Chester. As you watch the tape, think about this question: Are the Fines really fine?

Follow-up Questions:
1. So, is everything just fine with the Fines? Why do you say that?

2. What's the point of the gag about the elephant?

3. What do you think Serenity should do about Chip? How should she deal with him?

4. How do you think Serenity should have handled this situation of choosing the restaurant? What should she have said, and to whom?

5. Try a role play. Get four volunteers to play Serenity, Chip, Celeste, and Chester. Have Celeste start off with, "Well, Serenity dear, it's your birthday. Where do you want to go for dinner?" Then Chip chimes in, "I want pizza!" Then let the volunteers take it from there. Ask Serenity to deal with her family in the way she thinks is most biblical. The other three should try to stay in character, acting the way the characters on the video would act.

6.   a. Need some help from the Bible? Consider "speaking the truth in love" (Ephesians 4:15). Further along there's Ephesians 4:25–32.

   b. If you want to get in deeper, check out Romans 12:14–21. What would it look like for Serenity to bless Chip, not take revenge, but overcome evil with good? How could she be shrewd as a snake but innocent as a dove (Matthew 10:16)? This isn't doormat theology, this business of shrewdly overcoming evil with good. It requires strength and honesty coupled with gentleness, not spite. Is it more loving for Serenity to cheerfully go along with Chip's choice of restaurant, or to firmly choose another place and strongly but peacefully stand up to Chip? Why?

   c. Jesus was loving, but he never let himself be steamrolled. How did he pull it off? Read through Luke 20. How did Jesus handle manipulative, hostile people?

7.   a. Raise your hand if your family has an elephant in your living room that everyone pretends isn't there. Would you be able to tell the group about the elephant your family prefers to ignore?

   b. How does having an elephant in your living room make you feel?

   c. How would you describe your part in keeping the elephant in the living room?

   d. What does your family do to dust around the elephant in the living room? For example: Do you make excuses? Or cover up? Do you just not ever have friends over so you won't have to pretend?

   e. What would you like to do about that elephant? How does that compare with what you think you should do?

   f. Can the group help? How?

BIBLE STUDY:
1 Corinthians 1:18–2:5

There is serious disunity in the church at Corinth. Paul's starting point compares ordinary human wisdom with the extraordinary wisdom of God.

• Read or have someone read 1 Corinthians 1:18–2:5.
• Invite everyone to reflect for a moment on what they've heard as if they had never heard it before.

Talk:

1. What do you think of the flavor of this passage? Too sweet? Too bitter? Just right? Why?

2. How close is the description in 1 Corinthians 1:26 to our group?

3. Does it make sense to you that God would choose weakness instead of strength, foolishness instead of wisdom, to do his business in the world?

  a. Why do you say that?

  b. What light do verses 1:29–2:5 shed on God's motivation?

  c. What questions does this idea answer or raise for you?

2 Corinthians 12:1–10

Paul plays a word game with the Corinthian church. He is boasting—not about strength but about weakness—to persuade them to surrender themselves completely to God.

• Read or have someone read 2 Corinthians 12:1–10.

Talk:

1. What do you make of Paul's metaphor, "a thorn in my flesh"?

  a. What do you think he's getting at?

  b. Have you experienced anything like that?

Romans 7:14–25

Paul is writing to believers in the city of Rome. He's never met them and doesn't know if he ever will, so he gives them the honest stuff about everything that has to do with being a Christian—he tells them what he would show them if they were together.

• Read or have someone read Romans 7:14–25.

Talk:

1. If Paul talked like this when he was interviewing for a job as pastor of this church and you were on the interview committee, what would you be thinking? Why?

2. How close is this passage to your experience in trying to do the right thing?

3. Is it just me, or do Christians not talk much about the sort of thing we're reading here? Why do you think that is?

4. How do you feel about Paul's honesty?

    a. If you feel encouraged, why is that?

    b. If you feel discouraged, why is that?

5. Do you think this means it's futile to try to live like a Christian? Why?

READ:

"Is Christianity Hard or Easy?"

Read "Is Christianity Hard or Easy?" from *Mere Christianity* by C. S. Lewis (Macmillan Publishing Company; New York: 1952, pp. 166–169).

Talk:

1. What stands out for you in this passage?

2. How would you answer the question, "Is Christianity hard or easy?" Why?

3. Take a moment to reflect on your life. Have you given up trying to be good, or are you in the process—as Lewis says—"of becoming very unhappy indeed"?

TAKING STEPS:

Take time to make sure your group understands their action step assignments from the Student Journal. (See p. 6 in this guide and pp. 5–12 in the Student Journal.) The action step to emphasize this week is Action Step 5—Take out the trash. But you will also want to make sure your group is still tracking with Action Steps 1–4.

1. What's the most significant thing you've heard or thought in this session?

2. Why is that so significant to you?

3. What do you think you—or we—might do about that?

4. How can we be real? What can we do as a group to take out our trash?

Each Day This Week:
1. If we're going to be real, we're going to have to trust each other. Can we ask God to help us build absolute trust in each other? Pray the Pierced Ears Prayer using the words on page 7 of the Student Journal as a guide.

2. Will you make an effort to study the assigned Scripture passages and answer the questions in the journal this week?

3. Will you try to "catch the rave" and write down something good about our youth group or church every day this week?

Once This Week:
1. Read chapter 5 in Dan Lupton's book *I Like Church, But . . .*

2. Rave to a friend about youth group or church.

Before the Adventure Is Over:
1. Be real—take out the trash in your life.

PRAY:
Pray that our group will become a place where all of us can be real and really surrender our whole selves to Christ.

Notes

_____

_____

_____

_____

_____

_____

THEME 6

Session •6•

When Jesus is in the house . . . we make a difference

Days 35–41 in the Student Journal

GOALS:
• To celebrate people who make a difference
• To persuade your group that they can make a difference

VIEW:
In the House! Excerpts from EdgeTV
"E. V. Hill" from EdgeTV 9
Around 3 minutes

E. V. Hill is a bombshell pretty much everywhere he speaks, and this occasion was no exception. We're giving you a small piece of a longer speech he delivered to several thousand men. We think this story about the Black Panthers is so good it's a discussion starter all by itself.

For more than 30 years, Hill has been pastor of the Mount Zion Missionary Baptist Church in Los Angeles. During that time he's also been president of the L.A. Housing Authority, Honorary Consul General to the Republic of Liberia, a visiting professor at the California Graduate School of Theology, and has held several dozen other official posts, as well as building a couple of senior citizens' housing projects and generally being active in the L.A. community and around the world. Wow.

Focus Questions:
Before you turn on the tape ask: How capable of making a positive difference in the world do you feel you are? A lot capable? A little? Zip?

Follow-up Questions:
1. What are you thinking after watching that?

2. What are some of the things that push you to feel like you can't make a difference?

3. Paul told Timothy, "Don't let anyone look down on you because you are young, but set an example for the believers" (1 Timothy 4:12). Does being young make you feel you can't make much of a difference? Why do you say that?

4. David and Goliath (1 Samuel 17) is a classic tale of a teenager doing something by God's power that adults thought was impossible. After reading this, can you identify with David? Why or why not?

5. Gideon's story (Judges 6–8) is less known. To catch the humor, it helps to know the culture. The story opens when young Gideon is threshing wheat in a winepress because he doesn't want to be seen by roving gangs of Midianites. A winepress is deep, so the gangs can't see Gideon and come to steal his wheat. Now, threshing is separating the wheat grain from its chaff, its outer skin. Unfortunately, threshing involves tossing the wheat in the air with a rake and letting the wind blow the chaff away. You don't get much wind in a deep winepress, so threshing inside one is pretty pathetic work.

So while Gideon is driving himself nuts doing this because he's scared of the Midianites, an angel appears and says, "The Lord is with you, mighty warrior" (Judges 6:12). Excuse me? Gideon tries everything he can think of to get out of leading the Israelites against the gangs (all that stuff with the fleeces), but God is too smart for him.

You could tell the story of Gideon, reading some choice pieces, and ask your group to respond. A variety of questions could get the discussion started: How would it feel to be Gideon? Can you imagine doing what Gideon did? How many fleeces would it take to get you to tackle the Midianites? Who are your Midianites, and what will it take to get you to face them?

6. Another appropriate story is in 2 Kings 6:8–23, where Elisha shows his servant that the unseen forces of God are so much stronger than the visible forces attacking them. Verse 16 might be worth talking about.

7. The Jewish leaders were astonished that Jesus' disciples—"unschooled, ordinary men"—were so courageous in serving him (Acts 4:13). Acts 4 might be another passage worth looking at. What is courage? (Is courage shutting your eyes to risk?) Why were the disciples so brave? What would it take for you to act with such courage?

8. Don't get away from this discussion without getting practical. What could our group do to have an impact on non-Christians around us? How could we affect the lives of poor people in our community, for example, or of kids in our schools?

BIBLE STUDY:
Acts 4:1–21

You may remember the first 14 verses from the 27th day of this 50-Day Spiritual Adventure. Peter and John got mixed up with the Jewish authorities after they healed a 40-year-old paraplegic guy at the temple in Jerusalem. Needless to say, the event created a large, presumably unlawful, gathering.

• Read or have someone read Acts 4:1–21.
• Invite everyone to reflect for a moment on what they've heard as if they had never heard it before.

Talk:
1. What are your first impressions from this story?

2. Do you understand why the temple authorities were upset? Tell us what you think.

3. Try to think of something else that would create the same kind of reaction.
• Preaching the resurrection of Jesus in the Jewish temple would be like showing up at the New York Stock Exchange.
• Preaching the resurrection of Jesus in the Jewish temple would be like going to the British Parliament.
• Preaching the resurrection of Jesus in the Jewish temple would be like . . .

4. Look at verses 14–17: How would you describe the dilemma the Jewish leaders were in?

5. Why do you think they failed to persuade Peter and John to shut their yaps about the resurrection of Jesus? Look at verses 18–22 for clues.

6. Backtrack to verse 13: What set Peter and John apart from the crowd?
Is it just me, or does that seem remarkable to you? Why?

7. It's true, isn't it, that your schooling is unfinished? And we're all fairly ordinary here, are we not?

    a. So if anyone were going to be astonished by us—if we were going to make a difference in the world—what would they have to note about us?

    b. And is that true? Have we been with Jesus in an astonishing way? What makes you say that?

    c. What would it take for us to be with Jesus in a way that would make a greater difference in the world?

TAKING STEPS:

Take time to make sure your group understands their action step assignments from the Student Journal. (See p. 6 in this guide and pp. 5–12 in the Student Journal.) There is not a specific action step to emphasize this week. But you will want to make sure your group is still tracking with all the action steps.

1. What's the most significant thing you've heard or thought in this session?

2. Why is that so significant to you?

3. What do you think you—or we—might do about that?

4. How can our group make a difference (missions, community service, ecology)?

Each Day This Week:

1. You may not be able to change the whole world, but you can change the world for one other person by treating him or her as if he or she really mattered. Can we ask God to help us treat each other as if we mattered in this group? Pray the Pierced Ears Prayer using the words on page 7 of the Student Journal as a guide.

2. Will you make an effort to study the assigned Scripture passages and answer the questions in the journal this week?

3. Will you try to "catch the rave" and write down something good about our youth group or church every day this week?

Once This Week:

1. Read chapter 6 in Dan Lupton's book *I Like Church, But . . .*

2. Rave to a friend about youth group or church.

3. Cross the lines and get together with someone outside your normal circle.

Before the Adventure Is Over:

1. Cross the lines and get together with two people outside your normal circle of friends.

2. Electrify a friend and help bring out his or her potential.

3. Take out the trash in your life.

PRAY:

Pray that our group will learn to trust the power of Christ in us.

Notes

_____

_____

_____

_____

_____

_____

_____

_____

_____

_____

_____

_____

_____

_____

_____

_____

_____

_____

_____

_____

_____

_____

_____

_____

Session 7

THEME 7

When Jesus is in the house . . . God shows up

Days 42–46 in the Student Journal

GOAL:

• To sharpen your group's focus on knowing Christ intimately

READ:

"Jesus"

Read "Jesus" from *Good Advice* by Jim Hancock & Todd Temple (Youth Specialties; El Cajon, CA: 1987, pp. 72–74).

Jesus is God's way of saying "Yes!"

God created everything out of nothing, did it perfectly, and did it at his discretion. The far-flung galaxies dance in a great rhythm that God began because he wanted to. Nothing landed out of place when he spoke the world into being—not a flash of light, not a moment of time, not a speck of earth. Everything was perfect.

And he looked at it all so fondly and said, "Good!" And he looked at humankind, like looking in a mirror of sorts, and said, "Real good!"

And they all lived happily for about as long as it took for the humans to turn real good into real bad. Yet even then things weren't as bad as they could be. But when God looked at humankind again, the mirror was broken.

Some folks claim that the flaw in the whole system was God's big mistake in giving them (and, I suppose, us) a choice. But that was no fault. It was love.

God showed just what sort of person he is by entering creation through the broken glass and shattered image of the mirror. He became one of us! What a miracle—God becoming a squirming, crying, drooling, wetting, squalling baby boy! While King Herod had armed guards watching the front gate for uninvited guests, the real King of the Jews slipped unnoticed through the servants' entrance. Who could believe it?

God mended the broken image, made the glass shine like new, and he did it by becoming one of us—not less, not more, but completely human.

In Jesus Christ, God said, "Yes!" to the original plan, the only plan. Everything that went from good to bad got a brand new start in Jesus, and it's not because he had to do it. God chose to make the image right again because he wanted to, and he proved that the deed was done by the greatest feat of self-control creation has ever witnessed: "He made him who had no sin to be sin for us, so that in him we might become the righteousness of God."

Then he sealed the deal by raising the One who became sin for us right out of the grave forever, period.

What it means for you to "become the righteousness of God" has something to do with what it means to say "Yes!" to God.

Talk:

1. Does anything stand out for you from this reading? Why?

2. What do you think about the idea of "God becoming a squirming, crying, drooling, wetting, squalling baby boy"?

3. How easy is it for you to hear God saying "Yes!" to you? Why?

4. How convincingly have you said "Yes!" to God?

    a. Do you ever feel like taking it back? Why?

    b. Do you ever act as if you already took it back? How do you feel about that?

VIEW:

In The House! Excerpts from EdgeTV
"Old Friends"
7 or so minutes

"I believe I'm moving into the best years of my life."

Don Finto describes himself as a "radical confessor" and a "radical forgiver." In fact, for a guy who is 65 years old, he's pretty radical in many ways. Some of your group members may be close to their grandparents or to another older person, but some may have almost no relationships with anyone over sixty. That's unfortunate. Our culture sends the message that growing old is to be dreaded; we would like to explode that stereotype. And Don is just the man to do it.

Don started his working career as a college professor, but he's been the pastor of the Belmont Church in Nashville, Tennessee, for more than 30 years.

Focus Question:

Do you know anyone who's older than 60? What do you like about him or her? What do you not like?

Follow-up Questions:

As you listen to Don Finto, think about how you would describe him to someone who hasn't met him or seen this tape.

1. What are your overall impressions of Don?

2. Who in this group has a grandparent or another older person to talk to? How does that person make your life better?

3. Would you like Don as a grandparent or friend? Why or why not?

4. Why does Don think God was good to him even though he was molested sexually as a child? What do you think about that?

5. a. What do you think about forgiving people who don't even admit they were wrong?

   b. Don refers to Luke, where Jesus says, "Father, forgive them, for they do not know what they are doing." Notice that Jesus said this even though the soldiers and others were mocking him. Why would Jesus pray for people like that?

   c. When Jesus asked God to forgive these people, do you think he was saying what they did was okay?

   d. Do you think Jesus didn't care whether those people ever recognized what they did wrong? Do you think he doesn't care whether Don's father or molester ever recognize what they did wrong?

6. Don talked about being attracted to people who were passionate about Jesus. Do you know anybody like that? How do they affect you? What do you think is the secret to their passion?

7. Don said, "Whatever you can't get enough of is your god." What can't you get enough of? (This is a fairly threatening question. You might pass out pencils and cards and let students privately write down their answers. Then invite anyone to share who wishes to do so.)

8. When Don was younger, he didn't believe God could make him the man God said he could be. Do you believe God can make you a truly fabulous person? Explain.

9. Have you experienced becoming a better person by going through hard things? Tell us about it.

10. What do you think about the idea of confessing your stubborn sins to a friend? Why would that help you resist temptation?

11. Don decided divorce was no option for him. What do you think about that? Do you expect to get married someday? Do you expect to get divorced someday?

12. Why does Don think it's important to keep changing? Do you agree? Why or why not?

13. a. Don says things we refuse to deal with when we are young become the seats of horrible qualities when we are old. Have you ever known an older person with horrible qualities?

b. What kind of a person do you think you will be 50 years from now? Can you imagine yourself at that age? What might you be like?

14. What song does Don remind you of? What song would you sing or play for him if he were your friend?

BIBLE STUDY:
Philippians 3:1–11

It appears that someone said the Philippian Christians weren't really Christians at all. They said a person had to be a Jew before he could become a Christian. Solution? The Philippian men should convert to Judaism, get circumcised, and then make the jump to following Christ. Weird, huh? Well, Paul doesn't like it a bit.

• Read or have someone read Philippians 3:1–11.
• Invite everyone to reflect for a moment on what they've heard as if they had never heard it before.

Talk:
1. What is Paul's warning to the Philippians as this passage begins?

2. Why do you suppose he says: "It is we who are the circumcision, we who worship by the Spirit of God, who glory in Christ Jesus, and who put no confidence in the flesh"? Go to Jeremiah 9:25–26 and Romans 3:27–30 for clues.

3. In Philippians 3:4–6 Paul outlines the qualifications for boasting about his own religious excellence. Where does he go with that in verses 7–9?

a. Why do you think he turns the books upside down and calls his profit a loss?

b. Why do you think he would consider everything of value to be rubbish in order to gain Christ?

c. How common are these perspectives among the Christians you know? What do you think that says about us?

4. What is it that Paul wants in verse 10?

   a. Do you think Paul means the same thing most Christians mean when they say "I know Jesus"? Why?

   b. How important do you think it is to truly know Jesus? Go to John 17:1–3 for a clue.

5. Jeremiah 9:25–26 talks about God's punishment on those with uncircumcised hearts. Let's go back there to look at verses 23–24. What are your first thoughts about what God says here?

6. Why do you think people boast about wisdom, strength, or riches? What's wrong with that?

7. What are you most tempted to boast about? Why?

8. What do you think God means when he says that the only reason for boasting comes from understanding and knowing him?

9. In reality, just how well do you think you understand and know God? How do you feel about that?

10. What do you think it would take for you to understand and know God more deeply than you do today?

Write:
Take the next four minutes to write a note to God. What would you like to say to God about knowing him?

TAKING STEPS:
Take time to make sure your group understands their action step assignments from the Student Journal. (See p. 6 in this guide and pp. 5–12 in the Student Journal.) There is not a specific action step to emphasize this week. But you will want to make sure your group is still tracking with all the action steps.

1. What's the most significant thing you've heard or thought in this session?

2. Why is that so significant to you?

3. What do you think you—or we—might do about that?

4. How can we make sure God shows up in our group?

Each Day This Week:

1. When God shows up, he shows up for all of us. Can we ask God to help us treat each other as if we mattered to him? Pray the Pierced Ears Prayer using the words on page 7 of the Student Journal as a guide.

2. Will you make an effort to study the assigned Scripture passages and answer the questions in the journal this week?

3. Will you try to "catch the rave" and write down something good about our youth group or church every day this week?

Once This Week:

1. Read chapters 7–8 in Dan Lupton's book *I Like Church, But . . .*

2. Rave to a friend about youth group or church.

Before the Adventure Is Over:

1. Cross the lines and get together with two people outside your normal circle of friends.

2. Electrify a friend and help bring out his or her potential.

3. Take out the trash in your life.

PRAY:

Pray that our group will see Christ in a new way.

Notes

THEME 8

**When Jesus is in the hou͏
the future looks bright**

Days 47–50 in the Student Journ

GOAL:
• To finish the 50-Day Spiritual ͏ and celebration

VIEW:
*In the House! Excerpts from EdgeT͏
"Reuben" from EdgeTV 17
7 1/3 minutes

"The Lord wanted me to plant a seed—and I did."

Reuben's violent life may be a far cry from the lives of your group—or maybe not. In any event, making a stand for Christ and not fighting back is a challenge anybody can relate to. It's that old "turn the other cheek" thing. Still profoundly unpopular after all these years.

We think you'll find plenty to talk about once you've seen Reuben's courage and how love overcomes anger.

Focus Question:
Reuben makes a stand for Christ in the middle of a violent world. As you listen to Reuben's story, think about what motivates him.

Follow-up Questions:
1. a. What are your impressions of the overall picture of Reuben's high school years?

   b. What key words summarize Reuben's high school world?

2. When Reuben says he "had an attitude," what do you think he means?

3. Reuben appears to have made a radical transition in his approach to life. What do you think prompted the change?

4. How did you feel after watching this story?

5. What do you think about Reuben's response to the gang? Do you think you could make a stand like that if you were in his situation? Could you turn the other cheek?

6.   a. Reuben began praising and worshiping God during the confrontation. What do you think prompted that response?

   b. Compare Reuben's story to the account of the stoning of Stephen in Acts 7:54–60. (The first 53 verses record Stephen's reply to his accusers in the Jewish court.)

7. Reuben describes his actions as "planting a seed." What do you think he means by that? What could the seed grow into?

8.   a. Read Psalm 40:1–3. (You could play the song "40," from U2's *War* album and have everyone follow along from Psalm 40:1–3.) If this passage described Reuben, who would be the ones putting their trust in the Lord?

   b. Why do you think the Bible says "Many will see and fear"? What causes the fear?

9. Have you ever experienced the change from the mud to the rock? What happened?

10. Read 1 Corinthians 16:13. What do you think it means to do everything in love? How can you show courage and strength in love? How well do you think Reuben did at that?

11. What stand for Christ can you see yourself having to make? What could help you make that stand?

For Junior High Leaders:

You might take a little different approach to Reuben's story with junior high kids. We suggest focusing on questions 1.b., 2, 4, 10, and 11. Direct their attention to Reuben's stand and 1 Corinthians 16:13. Junior high boys may have a hard time understanding Reuben's response to the gang; if they can't buy his angle, that's okay. The seed is still planted.

BIBLE STUDY:
Jeremiah 29:4–14

The people of God have been dragged off to Babylon by the evil and egomaniacal Nebuchadnezzar. Though some expect God to liberate them any day now, Jeremiah says no, it's gonna be a long haul. This passage comes from the letter Jeremiah sent from Jerusalem to the surviving elders in Babylon.

• Read or have someone read Jeremiah 29:4–14.
• Invite everyone to reflect for a moment on what they've heard as if they had never heard it before.

Write:
Take the next two minutes to rewrite verses 4–8 in your own words.

Talk:
1. How would you describe the big idea in verses 4–8? *Get comfy! you're stayin*

2. Is there anything here that surprises or confuses you?

Verse 9 is a warning not to believe the false prophets who only tell people what they want to hear. Verses 10–14 are the real deal.

Write:
Take two more minutes to rewrite verses 10–14 in your own words.

Talk:
1. What do you think are the big ideas in verses 10–14?

After they call on Him, He will restore them back.

2. What questions or new insights do you get from these verses? *After 70 years,*

3. Look at verses 4, 7, and 14: *will they start calling on God after 70 years?*

   a. Who is ultimately responsible for God's people being stuck in Babylon?

   b. Is it just me, or is that a little scary? Why? Go to Jeremiah 25:1–14 for clues.

Let's pretend. What if Jeremiah 29 were a letter to our group, marooned on planet earth?

4. Looking at verses 4–9, how are we supposed to live for the next 70 years? Why?

5. How do you feel about that? Why?

6. Looking at verses 12–14, how are we supposed to relate to God for the next 70 years? How do you feel about that?

7. Looking at verses 10–11, how does God see the whole process? How do you feel about that?

1 John 3:1-3

This is the first of three letters John writes to talk about love, joy, and knowing Jesus.

• Read or have someone read 1 John 3:1–3.

Talk:

1. Why do you suppose John makes such a big deal about being called "children of God"?

2. Do you suppose you've placed as much importance on being called "children of God" as John apparently does? Why?

3. John says Christians are children of God now: What will we be? Why?

4. Has your life changed because of however much of Jesus you've seen so far?

   a. How much of Jesus do you suppose you have seen up to this point?

   b. How does that affect your attitude about seeing him "as he is"? What do you think that means?

5. What is the response that John expects from people who hope to see Jesus as he is? What do you think "purifying" means? Go to Titus 2:11–14 for clues.

Write:

Take the next four minutes to write a note to Jesus about seeing him face to face. How do you feel about that coming moment? Tell him about it.

TAKING STEPS:

Take time to make sure your group understands their action step assignments from the Student Journal. (See p. 6 in this guide and pp. 5–12 in the Student Journal.) There is not a specific action step to emphasize this week. But you will want to make sure your group is still tracking with all the action steps.

1. What's the most significant thing you've heard or thought in this session?

2. Why is that so significant to you?

3. What do you think you—or we—might do about that?

4. Does our group have a bright future?

Each Day This Week:

1. We're in this together! Can we ask God to help us treat each other as if we were destined to spend eternity with each other? Pray the Pierced Ears Prayer using the words on page 7 of the Student Journal as a guide.

2. Will you make an effort to continue to study Scripture? What would help you do that?

3. Will you continue to "catch the rave" and celebrate what God is doing here?

Once This Week:

1. Rave to a friend about youth group or church.

2. Get alone for a few minutes and ask God to electrify your life!

Before the Adventure Is Over:

1. Cross the lines and get together with two people outside your normal circle of friends.

2. Electrify a friend and help bring out his or her potential.

3. Take out the trash in your life.

PRAY:

Pray that our group will come to believe that God is in our future.

Notes

Notes

Additional Ideas

Here is a collection of ideas you might use instead of, or in addition to, the session plans. Or, use them for additional meetings. You can probably come up with an even better list of your own, but these ideas will get you off to a good start.

• What biographies have you read that apply to each topic? True stories of how people have let Jesus Christ affect all and turned their world inside out. Find relevant segments to read during sessions, or have volunteers read and report on various books. You may also be aware of films that will accomplish the same goal.

• Find a Bible character who represents each theme.

• Recruit someone in your church or neighborhood for a personal testimony. Teachers, athletes, business people, soldiers, pastors, retired people—look for someone who models the action steps.

• Do a special missions project to highlight the fact that, when Jesus is in the house, we make a difference. For hints on getting kids involved in missions and servant ministries, check out *Compassionate Kids* by Jim Hancock (Youth Specialties/Zondervan, 1995).

• Plan a retreat to celebrate the presence of Christ in your group.

• Cross the line with your whole group! Plan a joint meeting with a youth group that is very different from yours.

• If you are timing your Adventure to end on Easter Sunday (as many churches do), celebrate the resurrection of Jesus as God's greatest evidence that Jesus is *in the house!*

Last Words

Thanks for leading your group through the 50-Day Spiritual Adventure. I've been praying for you, and I would love to hear how it went.

At the end of these sessions, take a few minutes to reflect with your group on the 50-Day Adventure experience. Invite students to share what they liked most and what they liked least about the study. Ask which of the action steps they'd like to continue after the Adventure is over.

As you're completing this Adventure, The Chapel Ministries is already busy planning other 50-Day Adventures. They would appreciate input from your students regarding these Adventure materials. If possible, ask for written comments from the group, then send them to The Chapel Ministries.

And your feedback as a student leader helps in evaluating the effectiveness of the 50-Day Spiritual Adventure ministry. Please let The Chapel Ministries know what God did in your group during this 50-Day journey. Tell the story of how this Adventure has changed the lives of your students.

Send your comments to:

The Chapel Ministries
Editorial Department
Box 30
Wheaton, IL 60189-0030

or send an email to T50DSA@aol.com

For 50 days you and your kids have been studying the Bible and applying it to your lives. Why not encourage your kids to keep up with the action steps and habits they have formed during this Adventure? To help your kids stick with daily Bible study and prayer, Scripture Union has developed age-graded devotional study guides.

While the Adventure ends after 50 days, the habits your students develop don't need to. They can benefit from Scripture Union devotionals all year round! There are Scripture Union devotionals for young people of all ages. *One to One* is for youth ages 11–14, and *Discovery* is a personal application guide for mature young people and adults.

You may order Scripture Union devotionals by calling The Chapel Ministries at 1-800-224-2735 (1-800-461-4114 in Canada) or by filling out the order form on the back of this page.

Order Form for Scripture Union Guides

All devotionals will be sent every three months for one year.

❏ Yes! I would like annual subscriptions to:

	Price	Qty	Total
❏ Discovery	$20.00	_____	_____
❏ One to One	$20.00	_____	_____
		Grand Total	_____

Please fill out the information below:

Your Name _____

Church Name _____

Address _____

State/Prov _____Zip/Code _____Phone (___) _____

I'd like to pay by: ❏ Check ❏ Money Order ❏ VISA ❏ MasterCard ❏ Discover

Make checks payable to: The Chapel Ministries

Send this order form to:
The Chapel Ministries, Box 30, Wheaton, IL 60189
or call 1-800-224-2735 (in Canada 1-800-461-4114) for credit card order.

SLGSU97

If this Adventure has helped your students draw closer to God and develop healthy spiritual habits, then consider this other 50-Day Spiritual Adventure.

I'm So Confused!
Following Christ When Life Gets Crazy

Do your kids need to learn ways of applying God's wisdom to their current questions, to see how God leads them step by step, day after day, year after year for a lifetime? This 50-Day Spiritual Adventure will help your kids develop that step-by-step relationship with God and learn to live confidently in the confusion they face every day in the real world they live in.

Student Journal by Randy Petersen	$6.00*
When Life Become a Maze Guidebook by David Mains	$6.00*
Student Leader's Guide by Jim Hancock	$8.00
I'm So Confused: The Movie (EdgeTV)	$25.00

To order this 50-Day Spiritual Adventure, see the order form on the back of this page. If you are interested in other 50-Day Spiritual Adventures, call The Chapel Ministries at 1-800-224-2735 (1-800-461-4114 in Canada).

*See order form for quantity discounts.

THE CHAPEL MINISTRIES RESOURCES ORDER FORM

Item	Title	Price Ea.	Disc.	Qty	Total Amount
2720	*In The House* Student Journal	$6.00	**	_____	_____
1809	*I Like Church But . . .* Guidebook	$6.00	**	_____	_____
				Subtotal:	_____
450Y	*I Like Church But . . .* Audio Guidebook	$12.00		_____	_____
7796	*Make It Happen* Scripture Pack	$1.00		_____	_____
8427	*In The House: Excerpts from EdgeTV*	$25.00		_____	_____
				Subtotal:	_____
2620	*I'm So Confused!* Student Journal	$6.00	**	_____	_____
1761	*When Life Becomes a Maze Guidebook*	$6.00	**	_____	_____
				Subtotal:	_____
450U	*When Life Becomes a Maze* Audio Guidebook	$12.00		_____	_____
3606	*I'm So Confused!* Student Leader's Guide	$8.00		_____	_____
8420	*I'm So Confused: The Movie (EdgeTV)*	$25.00		_____	_____
				Subtotal:	_____
				TOTAL	_____

Add 10% for UPS shipping/handling ($4.00 minimum) _____

Canadian or Illinois residents add 7% GST/sales tax _____

Grand Total (Total + shipping + tax) _____

Here's my donation to help support the work of
The Chapel Ministries _____

Total Amount Enclosed _____

Ship my order to:

Your name _____

Church Name _____

Street Address* _____

State/Prov _____ Zip/Code _____ Phone _____

*(Note: UPS will not deliver to a PO box)

Mail this order form with your check made payable to:
The Chapel Ministries, Box 30, Wheaton, IL 60189-0030
In Canada: Box 2000, Waterdown, ON L0R 2H0

For Visa, MasterCard, and Discover orders call 1-800-224-2735.
In Canada call 1-800-461-4114.

** Quantity Discounts: 10–99 $4.95/100–299 $4.75/300+ $4.50   SLG97